KICKING & DREAMING

written by Jack Gates

illustrated by Estella Patrick

BELL ASTERI
PUBLISHING

Published by Bell Asteri Publishing
209 West 2nd Street #177
Fort Worth TX 76102
www.bellasteri.com

Published in the United States of America

ISBN: 978-1-957604-66-4 (paperback)
ISBN: 978-1-957604-67-1 (hardcover)

Jocelyn and Jayce,

"You girls are two of the strongest and bravest people I know. You both care so deeply about others and are always trying to help kids who are going through tough times, just like you did. You're an inspiration to us all, and I can't wait to see what the future holds for you two!"

From,
Jack

Ever since she was a little girl, Jocelyn knew she wanted to play soccer.

SHE PLAYED IN THE HOUSE...

IN THE BACKYARD...

AND AT SCHOOL WITH HER FRIENDS.

One day, Jocelyn felt very sick and had to go to the hospital in San Diego. The doctor came in and said she had something called leukemia.

He said she had to be very brave because it would take a long time for her to get better.

Jocelyn felt sad as she lay in the hospital, separated from her friends and the joys of playing outside. But while she was there, she met a new friend named Jayce, who was sick just like she was.

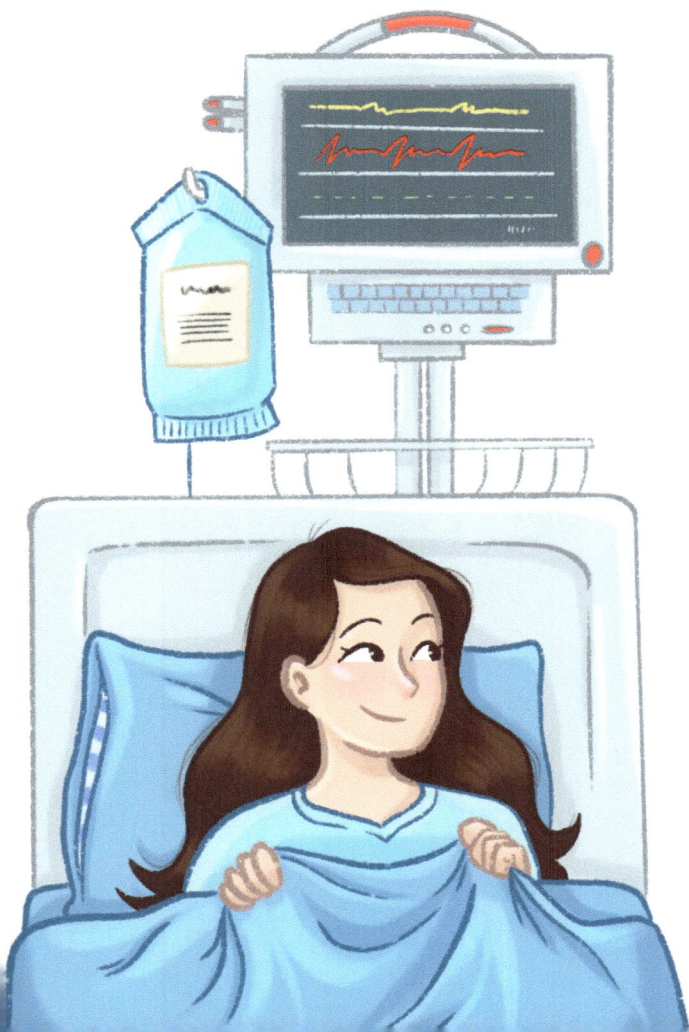

The dynamic duo became good friends, and they always looked forward to something they loved...

cheering on the USA soccer team while fangirling over their favorite player, **ALEX MORGAN!**

After a long journey, Jocelyn and Jayce were allowed to leave the hospital and go home because they started to feel better. It was nice to sleep in their own beds and see their pets again!

Jocelyn and Jayce enjoyed wonderful playdates together. They watched television, went swimming, and colored. They had so much fun together.

One day, their moms entered the room with exciting news. A professional soccer team was coming to San Diego, the place where they lived, and **ALEX MORGAN!** would be part of it!

AND THEY WOULD GET TO MEET THE TEAM BECAUSE OF THEIR INCREDIBLE BRAVERY AT THE HOSPITAL!

They arrived at the field to watch the team practicing, filled with excitement like never before. They were thrilled to see their favorite player in person!

While the team was practicing, Jocelyn and Jayce were kicking the ball along the side of the field. Alex approached the coach and quietly asked,

"WHO ARE THOSE GIRLS? THEY ARE REALLY GOOD!"

At the end of practice, the entire team gathered to chat with Jocelyn and Jayce. They presented them with a signed jersey, posed for photos, and shared valuable soccer tips.

As they were walking off the field, Alex approached them and said,

"YOU BOTH ARE IMPRESSIVE! KEEP PRACTICING, AND ONCE YOU FINISH YOUR TREATMENT AND FEEL BETTER, DON'T HESITATE TO GIVE COACH A CALL."

The girls tried to play it cool, but when they got to the car, they started jumping up and down and screaming,

"I CAN'T BELIVE THIS IS HAPPENING"

That next day, they started practicing together.

ALL DAY

&

ALL NIGHT.

A few months later, they went into the doctor's office for their final lab work. They had to sit and be brave. The doctor came in and said they were cancer-free! It was finally time to RING THE BELL!

Jocelyn and Jayce went straight to the field to play soccer. They were so happy, they ran around for hours pretending to be playing in a big stadium with the crowd cheering.

The next day, Jocelyn woke up and her foot hurt. She had a big bump and didn't know why. She called the doctor and he said that sometimes there are side effects after treatment.

Jayce said that she would be by her side until she felt better. They were upset that they couldn't play soccer, but they still had fun pretending and dreaming about playing with Alex Morgan and the

SAN DIEGO WAVE

To lift up her spirits, Jocelyn's mom got them tickets to go watch their favorite team play. They put on their jerseys, grabbed their signs, and they were ready to go!

After the game was over, they were able to go on the field and say hi to all of their new friends on the team!

Jocelyn and Jayce knew this was where they belonged.

Jocelyn was very patient and listened to her doctor. She was frustrated because she thought she would already be better.
It was good that she had a friend like Jayce to help her through it.

After weeks that felt like years, Jocleyn's foot finally felt better. It was time to call Coach. The girls were nervous but finally built up the courage to dial his number.

"Hi Girls, I've been waiting for your call! We have a big playoff game coming up and could really use you!"

That weekend, the girls got to the stadium together and got ready for the big game. They were nervous, but they knew they had each other. They had been through everything together.

Alex approached them and said, "You've made it through a lot of tough times together. I know you're going to do amazing today!"

It was time...

Jocelyn and Jayce locked hands with their favorite player and new friend, Alex Morgan, as they walked out onto the pitch.

Their hard work and bravery put them exactly where they had always wanted to be. Their dreams finally came true!

TRIUMPH TOGETHER

ABOUT THE AUTHOR

Jack Gates is 27 years old. While playing Division 1 hockey at Colorado College, he founded Triumph Together, a nonprofit organization that helps connect collegiate and professional athletes with kids at nearby children's hospitals by getting them tickets to games, meet and greets with players, signed gear, videos of encouragement before surgery, and much more!

Jack says, "Sports are special because they give people a sense of community, hope, and most importantly, something to believe in. That's what these kids need right now. They need something to look forward to, something to believe in, and to know someone is thinking of them during those extra tough days. We try and make up for lost time and give these kids experiences that they will never forget."

In 2023, Triumph Together merged with the Mitchell Thorp Foundation, a nonprofit that supports families whose children suffer from life-threatening illnesses by providing financial, emotional, and other resources to support their desperate situations.

Find out more...
www.triumphtogether.net (QR code on left)

ABOUT JOCELYN AND JAYCE

Jocelyn is a resilient and brave 13-year-old who started playing soccer when she was 5 years old but had to step away from the game when she was diagnosed with T-Cell Acute Lymphoblastic Leukemia at a young age. During the course of Jocelyn's 2.5-year journey, she went through 861 days of treatments, 22 lumbar punctures, 112 port access, 3 bone aspirations, 21 blood transfusions, 126 days of steroids, 65 days inpatient, 11 different types of chemo, and 7 chemo holds, but she never lost hope. Jocelyn finally rang the bell signifying the end of her treatments in January 2022. Just a short 6 months later, Jocelyn slipped back on her shinguards, tied up her cleats, and ran back onto a soccer field for the first time in almost three years, It was a great day!

After Jack Gates with Triumph Together heard that Jocelyn had the love of soccer and that her favorite player was Alex Morgan, he reached out to help make a manifestation into amazing reality with tickets to a San Diego Wave Soccer game, practice, and a meet and greet on the field with the whole team including Alex Morgan. Triumph Together has made memories of a lifetime for not only Jocelyn but for so many in our childhood cancer community.

Jayce was diagnosed with B-cell Acute Lymphoblastic Leukemia on April 24th, 2021, when she was 7 years old. Jayce's treatment lasted over 2 years. She took her last chemo pill on June 29, 2023, and "rang the bell," symbolizing the end of treatment. Jayce and Jocelyn became instant friends as they bonded over their similar experiences while fighting cancer. During treatment, Jayce was invited to attend a NWSL San Diego Wave game with Triumph Together, which sparked a newfound love of soccer.

Photos of Jocelyn, Jayce, and other friends from the hospital meeting Alex at practice and hanging out with the players down on the field after a San Diego Wave game

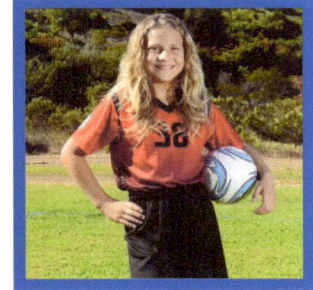

Photos of Jocelyn's last day of treatment and her playing soccer

Photos of Jayce ringing the bell and her in her soccer uniform

ABOUT THE ILLUSTRATOR

Estella Patrcik is no stranger to being a child with a serious illness. She was born with a congenital back condition, Spina Bifida, which resulted in her having three surgeries at 3 months, 10 years, and 15 years old. Her last two surgeries were at Cook Children's Hospital in Fort Worth, Texas. During her time at the hospital, she was encouraged to use art as a form of expression and a means of coping. Later, she became a published children's book illustrator with a focus on books that relate to childhood illness. She can be contacted via her website at www.alletsesart.com (QR code below):

www.ingramcontent.com/pod-product-compliance
Lightning Source LLC
LaVergne TN
LVHW072131070426
835513LV00002B/65

9781957604664